CLASSIC ROCK CLIMBS
NUMBER 08

THE DIAMOND of LONGS PEAK

ROCKY MOUNTAIN NATIONAL PARK, COLORADO

by
Richard Rossiter

T0346546

Chockstone Press
Evergreen, Colorado
1996

Classic Rock Climbs: The Diamond of Longs Peak, Rocky Mountain National Park, Colorado

This work is a derivative of Richard Rossiter's *Rocky Mountain Rock Climbs: The High Peaks,* **the second volume of a two-part series that includes** *Rocky Mountain Rock Climbs: The Crags.* **For more in-depth information to Rocky Mountain National Park, please consult these works. Both are published by Chockstone Press.**

Cover Photo: Richard Rossiter. All photos, unless noted, are by the author.

Design Consultant: Jack Atkinson.

Interior Design: Gloria Serena.

ISBN: 1-57540-025-1 *Classic Rock Climbs* series
1-57540-026-X *The Diamond of Longs Peak,*
Rocky Mountain National Park, Colorado

Published and distributed by
Chockstone Press, Inc.
Post Office Box 3505
Evergreen, CO 80437-3505

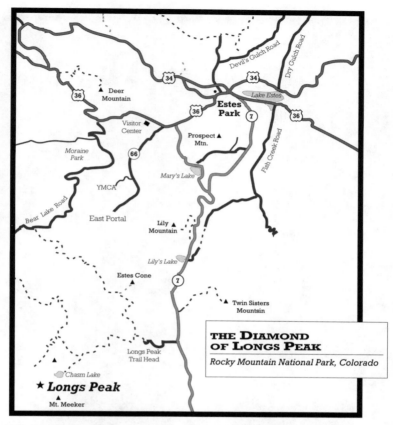

TABLE OF CONTENTS

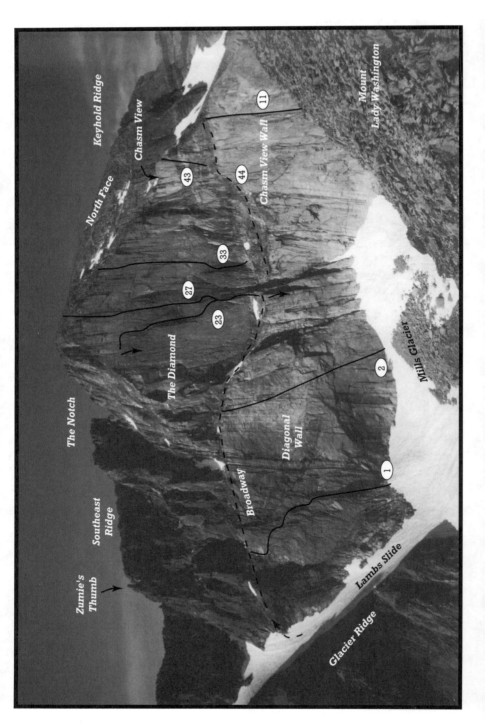

THE DIAMOND OF LONGS PEAK

ROCKY MOUNTAIN NATIONAL PARK, COLORADO

Longs Peak (14255) is the highest summit in Rocky Mountain National Park and perhaps the most characteristic landmark in Colorado. Its broad profile and flat top are visible from points all along the Front Range, though from the southeast, only the top can be seen above Mount Meeker. The first recorded ascent of Longs Peak was made by Major Powell and party during 1868.

This large, complex mountain is impressive from any view, but its most striking aspect is the east face. More than a mile wide and reaching a height of 1900 feet, the east face is home to such legendary features as The Diamond, The Diagonal Wall, and Chasm View Wall and is the premier arena for extreme alpine rock climbing in North America. High-standard forays such as *The Diagonal*, *D7*, *Yellow Wall* and *King of Swords* are known around the world. Yet the east face does not lack for high-quality mid-range action such as *Stettners Ledges*, *Directissima* and *Casual Route*.

PARK POLICY The high country of Rocky Mountain National Park supports a fragile ecosystem that is not immune to the intrusion of human beings. To preserve the alpine and tundra areas of the park, the National Park Service has found it necessary to develop a policy of limited use. Climbers do not need to register for ascents, but all overnight camps and bivouacs require a backcountry permit which must be obtained in person from the backcountry office or from a ranger station. There are strict regulations regarding fires, pets, the use of tents, et cetera. Make sure you are familiar with these policies before venturing into the backcountry…lest you be busted.

EQUIPMENT   Appropriate climbing hardware can vary drastically from one route to another and what a climber chooses to carry is a matter of style and experience. There is, however, at least in terms of crack width, a general array of devices that most parties would want to carry. Thus, a "standard rack" (SR) might consist of the following gear:

Set of RPs
Wired Stoppers up to one inch
2 or 3 slung Stoppers or Tri-cams
Various camming devices up to three inches
6 or 7 Quickdraws (QDs)
3 to 5 runners long enough to wear over the shoulder
1 double-length runner
6 to 8 unoccupied carabiners (usually with the runners)

On some routes this rack would be overkill; on others, it might be weak in certain areas. Snow and ice climbs typically will require crampons, ice axe(s), snow pickets or flukes and ice screws as well as some part of the rock climbing gear listed above and perhaps a few pitons. Equipment suggestions are given with some route descriptions; in some cases gear requirements are not known; otherwise, the gear listed above may serve as a general guideline.

RATINGS   The system used for rating difficulty in this book is a streamlined version of the so-called Yosemite Decimal System. That is, the Class Five designation is assumed, so that 5.0 through 5.14 is written as 0 through 14 without the 5. prefix. The Welzenbach classes 2 through 4 have been retained and appear in route descriptions as (cl3), (cl4) and appear with route names as Class 3 or Class 4. The Roman numeral grades I through VI for overall difficulty are also retained but are not applied to crag routes. The water ice rating system WI1 through WI6 is used for winter ice climbs. Alpine snow and ice climbs are rated AI1 through AI6. Mixed ice and rock is rated M1 through M6, a system initiated by Michael Bearzi.

The potential for a long leader fall is indicated by an "s" (serious) or "vs" (very serious) after the rating of difficulty. A climb rated "s" will have at least one notable run-out and the potential for a scary fall. A climb rated "vs" typically will have poor protection for hard moves and the potential for a very serious fall. The absence of these letters indicates a relatively safe climb providing it is within the leader's ability. Difficulty for runout sections is shown in italics when it is less than the maximum difficulty of a climb.

Note: The rating of a climb represents an informal consensus of opinion from some of the climbers who have completed a route. Some of the routes in this book may never have been repeated, which makes their ratings extremely subjective. But even the ratings of long established routes are debated, which indicates that numerical ratings have no absolute value and must be taken as approximations.

WEATHER AND SNOW CONDITIONS   Climbing in the high peaks is done primarily from June through September. During this period one can expect sunny mornings, comfortable to hot daytime temperatures and afternoon thundershowers. Until July, many peak climbs involve snow travel, whereas an ice axe and mountain boots may be useful for some part of the approach, climb or descent. From mid-July through August the weather is usually hot during the day and many climbs can be done without snow travel. Temperatures cool in September, but it is still reasonable to climb on warm days, even on The Diamond. By October the first serious snows come and windows of opportunity for rock climbing are rare; however, the alpine ice gullies are at their best. In November it gets cold and the winter ice climbs begin to form up. Winter ascents of the Diamond and other major features are not uncommon, but it's a whole different ball game than during summer. Spring is avalanche time in the Rockies.

A word of caution: Violent thunder storms with heavy precipitation including rain, hail and even snow are average fare during the summer. Which is to say, a warm sunny morning can go totally industrial by early afternoon. A climb should be started as early as possible so that one is off the route before the axe comes down. Sometimes the storms hit early and you get chopped anyway. Always carry storm gear.

ENVIRONMENTAL CONSIDERATIONS   Rocky Mountain National Park, which includes Lumpy Ridge, is one of the cleanest and best maintained parks in the country. To preserve the natural beauty and ecological integrity of our climbing environment, a few suggestions are offered.

Use restrooms or outdoor toilets where possible. Otherwise, deposit solid human waste far from the cliffs and away from paths of approach and descent. Do not cover solid waste with a rock but leave it exposed to the elements where it will deteriorate more quickly. Carry used toilet paper out in a plastic bag or use a stick or Douglas fir cone. Do not leave man-made riffraff laying about: If you pack it in, pack it out. Take care to preserve trees and other plants on approaches and climbs. Scree gullies and talus fields usually have sections that are more stable; thrashing up and down loose scree causes erosion and destroys plant life. Always use trails and footpaths where they have been developed and demonstrate human evolution by removing obstructions, stacking loose rocks along trail sides and picking up trash. When hiking across tundra, follow footpaths or step on rocks to avoid crushing the fragile plant life.

APPROACHES

East Longs Peak Trail—From Estes Park, drive 8.5 miles south on Highway 7 and turn west on a signed road that leads in one mile to the Longs Peak Campground and a ranger station. The trail begins just south of the ranger station and after 0.6 mile goes left at a junction with the Storm Pass Trail. At about 3.2 miles, the trail reaches a junction at Jim's Grove and goes left again. At 4.2 miles a third junction is reached below the east side of Mount Lady Washington. The left branch leads to Chasm Lake Cirque; the right branch to The Boulderfield.

Chasm Lake Trail—From the junction below Mount Lady Washington, follow the left branch for about 0.7 mile to its end at a patrol cabin below Chasm Lake. To reach the east face of Longs Peak, follow a vague path along the north shore of the lake and continue west to Mills Glacier which lies directly below the great east face. Note the following features: The Diagonal Wall is at left; Chasm View Wall at right. The narrow section between is the North Chimney area. Towering above is The Diamond. The long, curving ledge that separates The Diamond from the lower wall is Broadway. At the far left of the basin is the snow couloir of Lambs Slide.

Boulderfield Trail—From the junction below Mount Lady Washington, take the right branch which leads in a mile or so to Granite Pass (12090). At the pass is an intersection with the North Longs Peak Trail which begins from Bear Lake Road. Stay left and continue to the Boulderfield at 5.9 miles. From the Boulderfield, one has access to Chasm View, the north face of Longs Peak and The Keyhole (6.2 miles).

DESCENTS

The easiest descent from the summit is via The Keyhole. Though this is the long way around, it can be done safely without a rope. The next easiest is Clarks Arrow, which does not require a rope, but is steeper and less easy to follow. Neither of these routes is described in this book (see *Rocky Mountain National Park, The High Peaks* by Richard Rossiter, Chockstone Press 1996). The most efficient descent is the North Face: From the summit of Longs Peak, scramble down the north face to the steep slab just above Chasm View (cl4). Look for a cairn and a large iron eyebolt. This may be reached in a direct line from the summit, or more easily by descending the northwest ridge for several hundred feet, then curving around eastward to the same point. Rappel 150 feet from the eyebolt to steep snow or talus just above Chasm View. It is possible to rappel 75 feet twice using a second eyebolt halfway down. It also is possible to downclimb the 150 foot slab (4, wet). From here, one may scramble down talus to the Boulderfield or return to the Chasm Lake Cirque via The Camel. Note: An ice axe is recommended if the north face is covered with snow. Also: From the top of The Diamond it is not necessary to climb the last 200 feet to the summit, just traverse north to the North Face.

The Camel (Camel Slide)—The Camel is a large block on the ridge crest between Longs Peak and Mount Lady Washington that viewed from the north or south resembles a kneeling camel. To descend from Chasm View, hike east for a couple of hundred yards along the crest of the ridge to The Camel, then cross over to the south side of the crest. Work down and east across the south face of Mount Lady Washington to some grassy ledges at the head of a scree gully, then follow the gully southwest into the Chasm Lake Cirque.

RR The Diamond Rappel Route—From the top of *D7* (Almost Table Ledge), make five long rappels from fixed anchors to Broadway. The second and third anchors are on the route *Soma* to the left of *D7*. The fourth anchor is not on any route but has two bolts at a good stance. The fifth anchor is at the top of the first pitch of *Curving Vine*, from which a final rappel places one on Broadway. Walk north and down a bit to a bolt anchor with a chain at the top of the *Crack of Delight* (directly below the start to the *Casual Route*). Make four more long rappels from bolt anchors to Mills Glacier. None of the rappels exceed 150 feet but it is a good idea to knot the ends of the ropes.

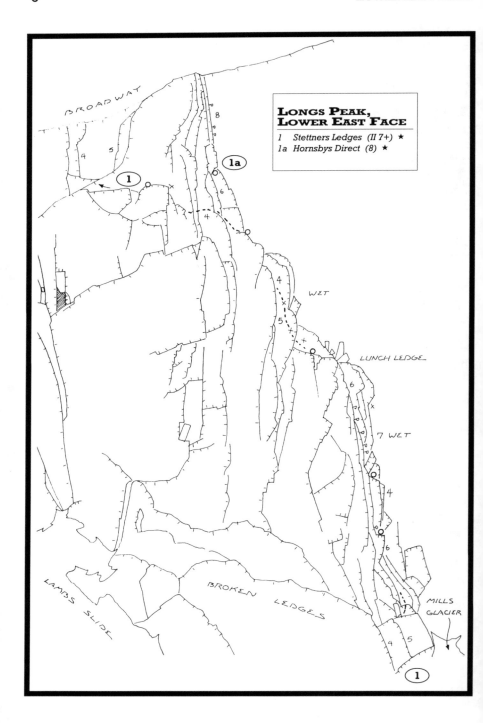

Longs Peak,
Lower East Face
1 Stettners Ledges (II 7+) ★
1a Hornsbys Direct (8) ★

SECTION ONE

LOWER EAST FACE

STETTNERS BUTTRESS

Stettners Buttress rises above the foot of Lambs Slide and defines the south edge of The Diagonal Wall.

1   **Stettners Ledges (II 7+)** ★   This famous route follows a long, right-facing dihedral system along the right margin of Stettners Buttress. It was a visionary climb at the time of its first ascent and today is one of the most popular climbs on Longs Peak. Kick steps up Mills Glacier about 200 feet right of Lambs Slide, then scramble up broken rock to the highest ledge beneath some right-facing dihedrals. **P1:** Climb a corner on the left (4) or right (6) to get started, then move right into a right-facing dihedral and climb to a small ledge with a fixed pin (6, 150 feet). **P2:** Climb around the right side of a flake, then go up a right-facing dihedral to a big ledge with a large flake (4, 90 feet). **P3a:** From the alcove formed by the flake, climb a steep corner with fixed pins (crux, often wet) and continue up a shallow dihedral with a two-inch crack. Belay on Lunch Ledge, a large terrace studded with big blocks. This lead is called The Piton Ladder (7+, 140 feet). **P3b:** From the right side of the big flake, climb a dihedral on the right all the way to Lunch Ledge (8). **P3c:** Climb the first twelve feet of The Piton Ladder, then swing left around the arête and climb ten feet to a grassy ledge (8). Continue up and left and climb to the top of a slab (6), then work right into the last 15 feet of the regular pitch. **P4:** Move the belay to the south end of Lunch Ledge. Climb a corner or steep flakes at left, then work up and left to belay on a ledge. **P5:** Traverse left and gain the end of a long ledge system (optional belay), then climb up and left and belay at a bolt (5). **P6:** Traverse left into a bowl or recess (optional belay), then climb the left side of the bowl to Broadway (4). FA: Paul and Joe Stettner, 1927.

1a Hornsbys Direct (8) ★ (This finish makes the climb a Grade III.) **P5:** From the top of the fourth pitch, follow shallow dihedrals up to a small ledge below a steeper section (6, 120 feet). **P6:** Follow a right-facing dihedral past a roof and many fixed pins to Broadway (8, 140 feet). The dihedral just to the left also may be climbed and is slightly more difficult. FA: Hornsby and Walton, 1949.

DIAGONAL WALL

This is the massive oval wall between Stettners Buttress and Fields Chimney. The following routes ascend the long diagonal crack system along the right side of the wall.

2 Diagonal Super Direct (V- 11d) ★ During the summer of 1987, Roger Briggs and Chip Chase climbed The Diagonal crack system without any detours all the way to Broadway. This was the last of all the variations to the original route and the only one to stay with the crack. It is in a sense the true *Diagonal* and is the recommended version of the route. Briggs and Chase speculated that this was the line Kor had followed in 1963, but this is not supported by the description in Walter Fricke's guidebook. The long and beautiful final pitch, which was likely unclimbed previously, is the crux of the route. Their ascent required five-and-a-half hours.

3 Diagonal Direct (V- 11c/d) ★ This variation to the original route follows the *Diagonal* crack system for five pitches, then makes a rightward traverse into a long, right-facing dihedral that is followed to Broadway. The traverse on the first ascent nailed right beneath an arch; the free version takes a higher line as shown in the topo. FA: Layton Kor and Tex Bossier, 1963. FFA: Jeff Achey and Charlie Fowler, 1980.

4 The Diagonal (V 9 A3) This historic route ascends the long diagonal crack system to the right of the arching roofs. It was the first major wall climb completed on the east face of Longs Peak and set the ground for the first ascent of The Diamond a year later. The original line is marked on the topo, but is rarely climbed. FA: Ray Northcutt and Layton Kor, 1959.

5 Directagonal (V- 11c, *9vs*) ★ This is the first free version of *The Diagonal*, which breaks right lower on the wall and rejoins the original route after the rappel/pendulum. Climb the first pitch and a half of the regular line, then traverse right at a dark band (7) and proceed as shown in the topo. FFA/FA: Roger and Bill Briggs, 1977.

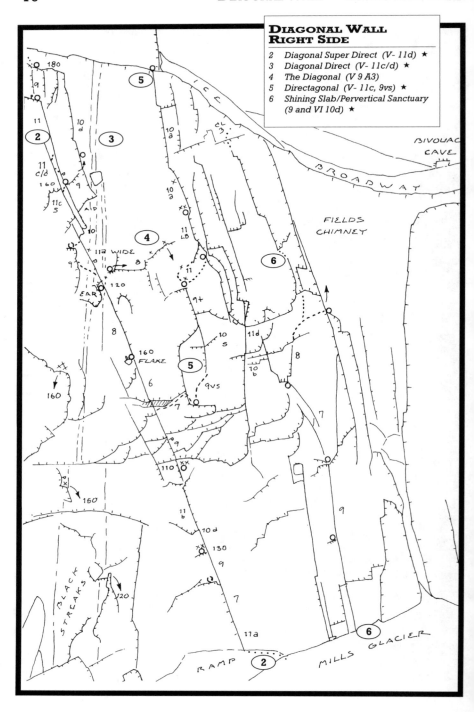

DIAGONAL WALL RIGHT SIDE

2   Diagonal Super Direct (V- 11d) ★
3   Diagonal Direct (V- 11c/d) ★
4   The Diagonal (V 9 A3)
5   Directagonal (V- 11c, 9vs) ★
6   Shining Slab/Pervertical Sanctuary
    (9 and VI 10d) ★

6   **Shining Slab/Pervertical Sanctuary (9 and VI 10d)** ★   This is the lower section of the acclaimed Diamond route Pervertical Sanctuary. The first ascent is thought to have begun with *Shining Slab*, then passed through a break in the right side of the big roofs and finished in the left-facing dihedrals to the right of the Grey Pillar. FA: Ron Olevsky and Bob Dobbs (original rating unknown), Winter 1974. FFA: Unknown.

7   **Crack of Delight (II+ 7)**   This route ascends a flower-filled crack and chimney system about 100 feet left of the North Chimney. It is not often climbed, but is included here as an aid in locating the lower part of the *Diamond Rappel Route*, which begins from the top of *Crack of Delight*. FA: Layton Kor and Tex Bossier, 1963.

8   **La Dolce Vita (VI 8 A4)**   This is the lower section of an aid climb that ascends the entire east face from Mills Glacier. Climb the first two pitches of *Crack of Delight*, but where that route goes left, continue straight up the dihedral. Eventually veer right and climb the upper North Chimney to Broadway. *La Dolce Vita* has been published elsewhere as a winter climb and the first Grade VI route on the east face, however, according to Charlie Fowler, the route was climbed in June. Note that The Diamond route *Pervertical Sanctuary* was begun from Mills Glacier during the winter of 1974; the original rating is unknown but the ascent would have been a Grade VI. FA: Charlie Fowler and Renatto Casaratto, 1984.

9   **North Chimney (4 or M3)**   This is the conspicuous, deep chimney beneath the center of The Diamond. It is the right of two large chimneys, the left being Fields. The amount and density of snow in the chimney varies with season. The *North Chimney* offers the most direct approach to routes on The Diamond but is made less attractive by the necessity of snow travel and random rockfall. During summer it is steep and wet with loose rock and has been the scene of some nasty accidents. The chimney is often soloed to save time but conditions and experience may warrant belays. FA: E.H. Bruns and W.F. Ervin, 1925; according to Walter Fricke, it was soloed by Bruns, 1925.

CHASM VIEW WALL

This is the broad reddish wall around to the right from the North Chimney. The top of the 600-foot wall forms the connecting ridge between Longs Peak and Mount Lady Washington.

Approach: Hike in via the East Longs Peak Trail and take the left branch into the Chasm Lake Cirque. Hike over boulders along the north shore of the lake, then contour around to the far north side of Mills Glacier. Scramble up a series of ramps to a ledge system at the bottom of the steep face (cl4).

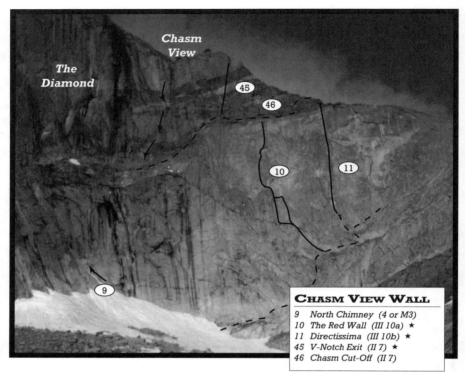

The Diamond

Chasm View

45

46

10

11

9

CHASM VIEW WALL

9   North Chimney (4 or M3)
10 The Red Wall (III 10a) ★
11 Directissima (III 10b) ★
45 V-Notch Exit (II 7) ★
46 Chasm Cut-Off (II 7)

10 **The Red Wall (III 10a)** ★   This route is very steep and
continuously interesting. Identify a series of right-facing flake-
dihedrals to the left of the more obvious *Directissima* in the center of
the wall (below). From the north side of Mills Glacier, scramble up a
ramp to the grassy ledges in the middle of the wall (cl4). A smooth
gray ramp slants up to the left. Hike about 40 feet up the ramp and
belay. To finish, traverse right and finish with the *Chasm Cut-off* or
scramble up and left and climb *V-Notch*. FA: Layton Kor and Tex
Bossier, 1963. FFA: Unknown.

11 **Directissima (III 10b)** ★   This classic is an imperative for the wide
crack enthusiast. Identify a vertical, right-facing flake-dihedral
system that tops out at the right end of the dark rock at the top of the
wall. The crux is at a roof on the fourth pitch but the squeeze
chimney on the third will burn more calories. Scramble up the ramp
as for *The Red Wall* but continue up and right to the highest ledges at
the bottom of the *Directissima* crack system. Starts up an obvious,
flower-filled right-facing dihedral that leads to a ramp beneath a
small roof. Pro: SR plus an extra #3.5 and #4 Friend. FA: Layton Kor
and Bob LaGrange (III 5.8 A2), 1960. FFA: Roger Briggs and Chris
Reveley, 1974.

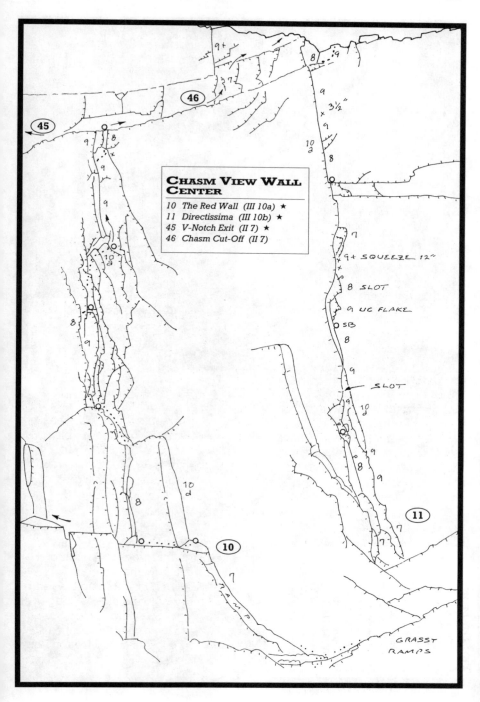

CHASM VIEW WALL CENTER

10 The Red Wall (III 10a) ★
11 Directissima (III 10b) ★
45 V-Notch Exit (II 7) ★
46 Chasm Cut-Off (II 7)

THE DIAMOND

A	Kiener's (4)
9	North Chimney (4 or M3)
13	Pervertical Sanctuary (IV+ 11a) ★
18	D7 (V- 11c) ★
20	Yellow Wall (V- 10d or 11b) ★
25	Casual Route (IV 10a, 7s) ★
28	D1 (V 12a/b) ★
35	King of Swords (V 12a, 11a s) ★
38	The Joker (V 12c) ★
41	Waterhole #3 (V 5 A2)
42	Diamond Star Halo (V 9 A4)

SECTION TWO

THE DIAMOND

The Diamond is the most famous alpine wall in the United States. Its imposing plane towers above Chasm Lake like a giant drive-in movie screen—one million square feet of rock hanging in the sky. The big wall faces northeast and lies between 13,000 and 14,000 feet, its top a mere stroll from the summit of Longs Peak. It is dead vertical to overhanging, remote, bloody cold and is blind to storms approaching from the west. Just peering up at the looming face from broadway stimulates the imagination, if not second thoughts. To climb any route on The Diamond is a formidable challenge and should not be taken lightly. The sun leaves the face at about 11:00 a.m., after which the temperature plummets. Storm gear must be carried and speed of ascent is essential.

The Diamond is host to 34 major routes, of which only 18 have been climbed free. All routes follow the long vertical crack systems that characterize Diamond climbing. The rock on the left side of the wall is generally very good and most of the routes are free climbs. The rock on the right side is steeper and somewhat rotten and most of the routes are aid climbs. Some ascents can be completed car-to-car in a long arduous day, but because of the approach distance, altitude and severity of the routes, some parties will want to bivouac. Standard sites are in the boulders below Mills Glacier, on Broadway and at Chasm View. The park service limits the number of people who can stay overnight at these locations. All but two routes begin from Broadway, the long ledge that runs across the bottom of the wall.

APPROACHES AND FINISHES

Approach A—Chasm Lake Cirque: This approach requires an ascent of Mills Glacier and a route on the Lower East Face to reach Broadway. The *North Chimney* provides the most expedient passage. Any of the longer routes such as *The Diagonal* or *The Grey Pillar* will turn the ascent into a Grade VI. It is possible to climb *Lambs Slide* and traverse back north along Broadway, but this involves considerable snow travel and is seldom done.

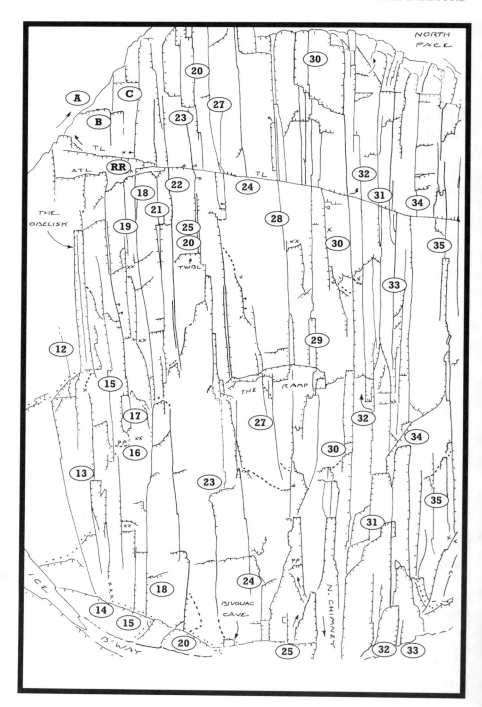

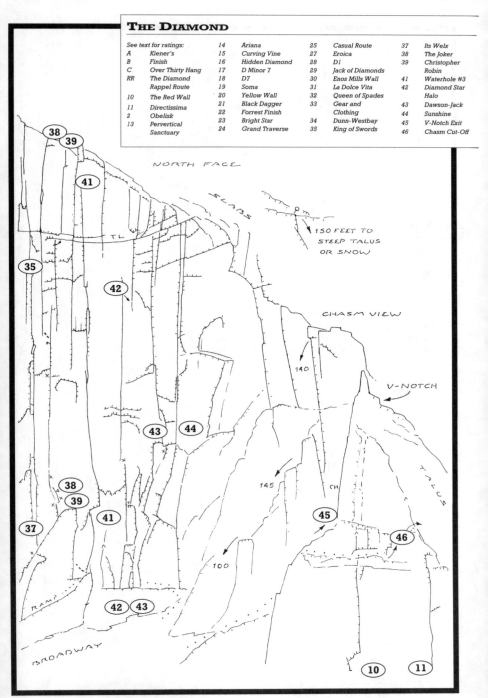

THE DIAMOND

NORTH FACE

SLABS

TL

150 FEET TO STEEP TALUS OR SNOW

CHASM VIEW

140

V-NOTCH

145

CH

TALUS

100

RAMP

BROADWAY

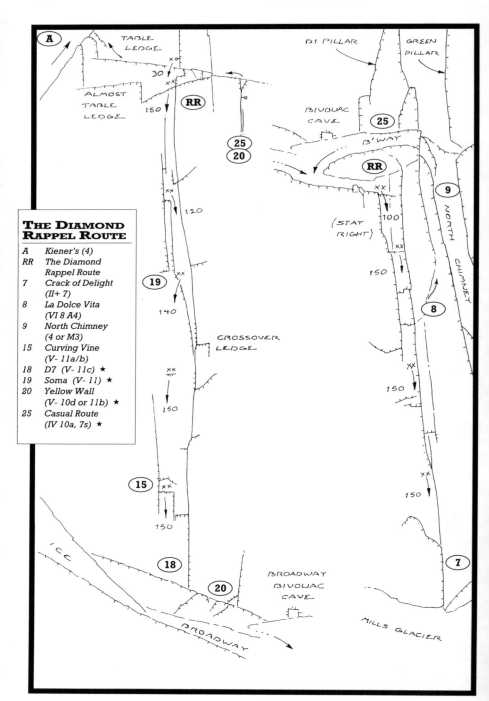

**THE DIAMOND
RAPPEL ROUTE**

A   Kiener's (4)
RR   The Diamond
     Rappel Route
7   Crack of Delight
     (II+ 7)
8   La Dolce Vita
     (VI 8 A4)
9   North Chimney
     (4 or M3)
15   Curving Vine
     (V- 11a/b)
18   D7 (V- 11c) ★
19   Soma (V- 11) ★
20   Yellow Wall
     (V- 10d or 11b) ★
25   Casual Route
     (IV 10a, 7s) ★

Approach B—Chasm View: The least dangerous but more roundabout way to reach Broadway is to rappel from Chasm View. From the Boulderfield, hike up talus to Chasm View (13529), the notch at the far right corner of The Diamond and make three long rappels to the north end of Broadway.

Table Ledge is a long, horizontal crack system that runs across the upper part of The Diamond. Every route ends at this crack or crosses it. The far south end of the crack forms a grassy bench where one can exit left to *Kiener's.* The remainder of the crack is not a ledge. About 30 feet below the left end of Table Ledge is another narrow bench called Almost Table Ledge. There are three ways to finish a climb from the bench at the south end of Table Ledge crack:

Finish A—Kiener's (4): Traverse left on Table Ledge and gain a long talus slope that runs along the south edge of The Diamond. This is the upper part of a mountaineering route called *Kiener's.* Hike up the slope and continue as it narrows into a gully. Skirt around the base of a buttress and reach a broken slope above the top of The Diamond. Scramble 200 feet to the summit, or traverse northwest and descend the North Face.

Finish B—From the middle of Table Ledge, climb either of two cracks to the top of the face and join *Kiener's* (7, 120 feet).

Finish C—Over Thirty Hang (7 A2): From the bolt belay on Table Ledge, climb a left-facing dihedral and belay beneath a large overhang (130 feet). Aid left beneath the roof for twenty feet, then climb thirty feet straight up to the top of the face. The six-inch crack through the roof may have been free climbed. FA: George Hurley and Jonathan Hough, 1967.

THE OBELISK AREA

The Obelisk is a 210-foot pillar at the upper left side of The Diamond. Three excellent routes ascend this narrow column and converge at Obelisk Ledge at its top. A final pitch, the original last pitch of Curving Vine (9), leads to Almost Table Ledge whence one may continue to Table Ledge and Kiener's, or traverse right to Diamond Rappel Route.

12 **Obelisk   (IV+ 11b/c)** ★   This route climbs the great white left-facing dihedral along the left side of the Obelisk pillar. The final pitch ascends a slightly overhanging five to six-inch slot. Begin from the top of an ice patch at the far left corner of The Diamond. Climb a right-facing dihedral (7, *Window Direct*), then follow ramps up and right for two pitches (4) to a sloping ledge at the base of the Obelisk dihedral. The Obelisk may also be started with the first three pitches of *Pervertical Sanctuary.* **P1:** Climb a long handcrack and belay at a stance with two bolts (11, 100 feet). **P2:** Continue up the corner and belay at the base of the final offwidth (10a, 35 feet). **P3:** Climb the awesome slot which may be partly protected by small nuts on the

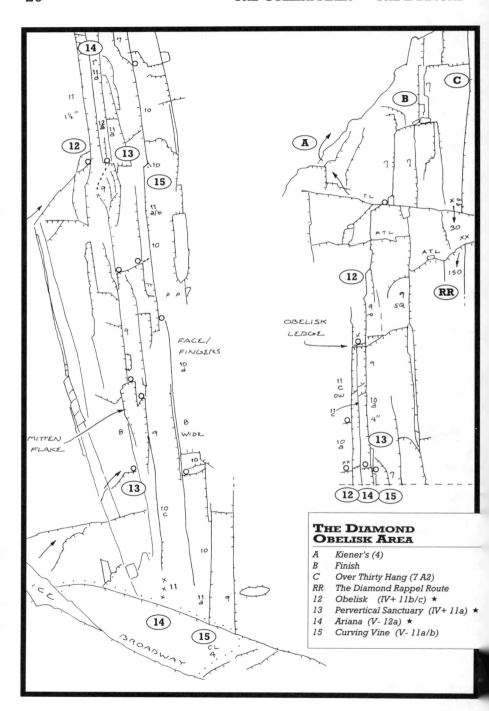

THE DIAMOND OBELISK AREA

A   Kiener's (4)
B   Finish
C   Over Thirty Hang (7 A2)
RR   The Diamond Rappel Route
12   Obelisk   (IV+ 11b/c) ★
13   Pervertical Sanctuary (IV+ 11a) ★
14   Ariana (V- 12a) ★
15   Curving Vine (V- 11a/b)

inside and belay on Obelisk Ledge (11, 75 feet). **P4:** From the right side of the pillar, follow a steep crack to Table Ledge (9, 130 feet). Pro: SR plus some offwidth gear. FA: George Hurley, 1974. FFA: Chris Reveley, 1977.

13 **Pervertical Sanctuary (IV+ 11a)** ★ This popular tour ascends a crack system up the far left side of The Diamond and finishes with two excellent pitches (fingers to fist) up the right side of The Obelisk. A point of identification is the Mitten Flake, a large flake about 100 feet above Broadway that is reminiscent of a Dachstein mitt with the thumb on the right. Begin near the bottom of an icefield at the lower left side of The Diamond. **P1:** Work in from the left and climb the left side of the Mitten Flake to a belay at its top (8, 130 feet). **P2:** Climb the crack above the Mitten and belay on a ledge at right (9, 100 feet). **P3:** Climb the crack and left-facing corner to where it veers left, then work up and right past a bolt and gain the ledge at the bottom right side of The Obelisk (9, 100 feet). **P4:** Jam a difficult handcrack and belay on a wedged block (11a, 130 feet). **P5:** Jam up the four-inch crack in the right-facing corner along the right side of The Obelisk and belay at the top of the pillar (10a, 80 feet). **P6:** From the right side of the pillar, follow a steep crack to Table Ledge (9, 130 feet). Pro: SR plus extra gear from one to four inches. FA: This is The Diamond section of a long aid route by Ron Olevsky and Bob Dodds that began from Mills Glacier with *Shining Slab*, 1974. FFA: Bruce Adams and Tobin Sorensen, 1975.

14 **Ariana (V- 12a)** ★ This route ascends a long, thin crack up the middle of The Obelisk. The fourth pitch is the crux and is well-protected. Pro: SR with extra Stoppers and small cams. Begin up on a ledge below three bolts, to the right of the start to *Pervertical Sanctuary*. FA: George Hurley, 1975. FFA: of entire free line, Roger Briggs, 1985.

THE YELLOW WALL AREA

This section of The Diamond lies between The Obelisk (at left) and the Grand Traverse Dihedral. The very flat wall is characterized by long, thin cracks, an abundance of face holds and small ledges. At the bottom right of this area, directly beneath the Grand Traverse Dihedral, is a small, square-cut inset called the Broadway Bivouac Cave. If not the Longs Peak Hyatt, it is at least a good point of reference.

15 **Curving Vine (V- 11a/b)** The route shown in the topo is the free version. The original line made a pendulum on the first pitch to gain the long crack that is the main feature of the route. About 200 feet below Table Ledge, the crack fades and a second pendulum was made into the crack that is now the fifth pitch of *Ariana*. The free version goes left well below this pendulum and finishes with the fifth pitch of *Pervertical Sanctuary*. Begin in the first crack system to the

right of the bolt ladder on *Ariana*, about 20 feet left of the start to *D7*. It is possible to climb the first 90 feet of *D7* and traverse left on a ledge to join the route (9). Pro: Slightly enhanced SR. FA: Michael Covington and Pete Robinson (V 5.6 A3), 1966. FFA: Unknown.

16 **Hidden Diamond (V- 11d)** ★   This difficult route begins with the first two pitches of *Curving Vine*, traverses right to join *D Minor 7* for two pitches, then continues straight up where the latter veers off to the right. The crux fourth pitch includes a fist crack followed by a strenuous knifeblade crack. Pro: Rack up to four inches with extra RPs or equivalent. FA: Ed Webster and Robert Anderson, 1985. FFA: Ed Webster and Pete Athens, 1985.

17 **D Minor 7 (V- 11d)**   This is an early aid route that has been confused with the *D7 Variation* above Crossover Ledge. Fortunately, Bob Bradley contributed a large marked photograph of The Diamond that clearly shows this route—it is also described correctly in Walter Fricke's old guide. It begins with the first 130 feet of *Curving Vine*, jogs right to follow *D7* for 200 feet, then angles up and left for 120 feet into a crack system that is now shared with the third and fourth pitches of *Hidden Diamond*. At a point slightly lower than the Yellow Wall Bivouac Ledge, *D Minor 7* again jogs right into the next crack system (*Soma*) and continues to Almost Table Ledge. FA: Bob Bradley and Rick Petrillo (V 5.7 A3), 1967. The section of the climb between *D7* and *Hidden Diamond* as well as the final pitch were climbed free during 1994 by Roger Briggs.

Crossover Ledge spans 25 feet between D7 and the Yellow Wall about 320 feet above Broadway. It provides a belay for Soma, D7, Black Dagger, Forrest Finish and the Yellow Wall. It can be reached in two long leads via D7, which allows a very rapid start to any of these routes.

18 **D7 (V- 11c)** ★   *D7* features beautiful, solid rock and good cracks all the way up; it is one of the best routes on Longs Peak. As an aid climb, it was the easiest and most popular route on the wall (V 5.6 A2) and was generally considered the best candidate for the first free ascent of The Diamond, however, the final smooth head wall below Table Ledge rebuffed all attempts. In 1975, Wayne Goss and Jim Logan made the first free ascent of The Diamond by climbing the first three pitches, then traversing right into the *Forrest Finish* and on to Table Ledge via the last pitch of *Black Dagger*. Two years later, John Bachar climbed *D7* all the way to Table Ledge and unveiled one of the finest free climbs in the park. Begin at the second left-facing dihedral left of the Broadway Bivouac Cave and scramble through a broken rock band to a ledge at its base. **P1 and 2:** Follow a continuous crack for two long pitches of ascending difficulty and belay on Crossover Ledge (9 to 10b, 320 feet). Traditionally, this section is climbed in three pitches. **P3:** The prominent right-facing dihedral that proceeds from the left end of the ledge is not the

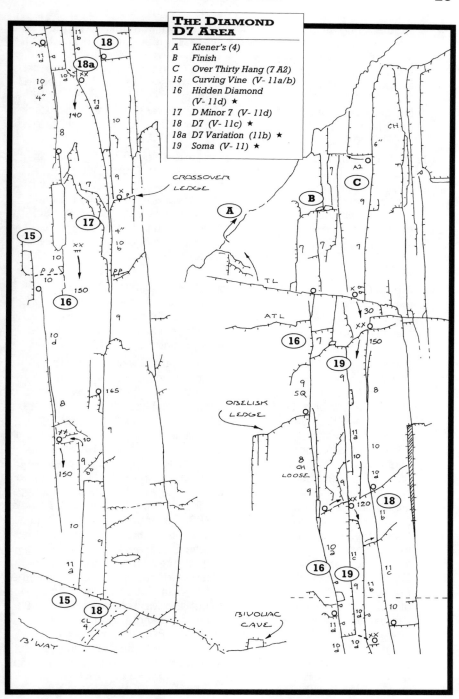

THE DIAMOND D7 AREA

- A   Kiener's (4)
- B   Finish
- C   Over Thirty Hang (7 A2)
- 15   Curving Vine (V- 11a/b)
- 16   Hidden Diamond (V- 11d) ★
- 17   D Minor 7 (V- 11d)
- 18   D7 (V- 11c) ★
- 18a   D7 Variation (11b) ★
- 19   Soma (V- 11) ★

standard line and leads into the *D7 Variation* (see below). Climb the smaller right-facing corner and crack a few feet right of this and gain a sloping ledge (10d, 115 feet). **P4:** Climb three parallel cracks to another small ledge (11c, 115 feet). **P5:** Climb a thin crack that widens to about ten inches and continue more easily to Almost Table Ledge (11a, 130 feet). **P6:** Climb a short pitch up and right to reach Table Ledge, then traverse left about 20 feet to belay (8, 50 feet). Pro: Rack up to four inches. FA: Larry Dalke, Wayne Goss and George Hurley, 1966. FFA: John Bachar, 1977.

18a **D7 Variation (11b)** ★ Also known as the Head Wall Bypass, this provides a slightly easier finish to *D7*. From **P4:** From Crossover Ledge, climb the left of two right-facing dihedrals or climb 50 feet of D7 and step left into the line. Follow a thin crack as it veers left and belay at a stance with two bolts (11a, 110 feet). **P5:** Climb the crack (which now goes straight up) for 75 feet, then traverse right on a sloping ledge and continue with the fifth pitch of *D7* just above the crux (11b, 150 feet). It may be possible to move up and left from the end of this pitch and finish with *Soma*.

19 **Soma (V- 11)** ★ This hybrid route begins with the *D7 Variation*, explores a previously unclimbed dihedral and finishes with the final pitch of *D Minor 7*. Part of the crack on the fifth pitch is filled with beautiful alpine flowers. These fragile plants can be spared by face climbing around them. FA: Roger Briggs and Michael Gilbert, 1994.

20 **Yellow Wall (V- 10d or 11b)** ★ This magnificent line was the second route completed on The Diamond and is among the most coveted alpine rock climbs in North America. It has two high-standard variations, of which the *Briggs-Candelaria* is the most frequented and is described here as the standard line of the route. From the Broadway Bivouac Cave, scramble up and left along a ramp for about 75 feet to the bottom of a shallow left-facing dihedral. **P1a:** Work up and right across the face, then up and left to gain the crack above the dihedral (7). Continue to the top of the crack, then work up and left to belay at the base of another crack (9, 120 feet). **P1b:** Climb the left-facing dihedral to the same fate (11a/b, 120 feet). **P2:** Climb the crack to a stance on the right (9, 130 feet). **P3:** Continue up the crack and shallow left-facing dihedral (often wet), then make a difficult move left to Crossover Ledge (10d, 120 feet). **P4:** Climb a left-facing dihedral above the right end of the ledge, then move right into the *Black Dagger* crack system. Climb a few feet, then move right again into the *Forrest Finish* crack and climb to a semi-sling belay beneath an offwidth section (9, 100 feet). **P5:** Climb the wide section (8, up to 12 inches) and continue up the crack of varying width, then break right along a ramp and belay on the Yellow Wall Bivouac Ledge (10b, 160 feet). **P6:** From the right side of the ledge, climb an inset (9+) followed by a narrow chimney (8), then pass a bulge with a fixed pin (crux) and belay at Table Ledge (10a, 130 feet). From here it is possible to

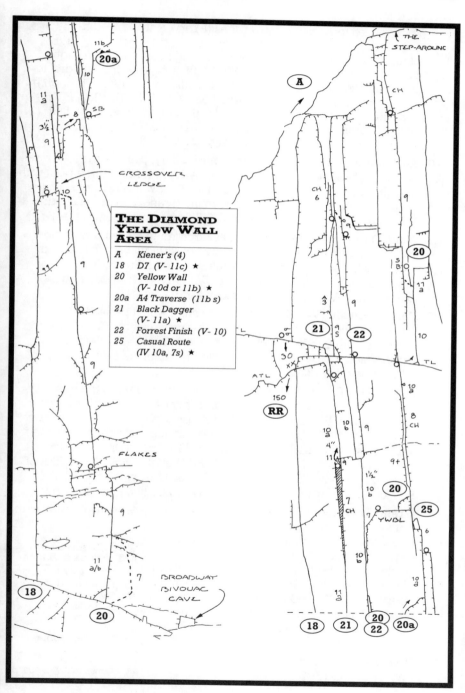

THE DIAMOND
YELLOW WALL
AREA

A   Kiener's (4)
18   D7 (V- 11c) ★
20   Yellow Wall
     (V- 10d or 11b) ★
20a A4 Traverse (11b s)
21   Black Dagger
     (V- 11a) ★
22   Forrest Finish (V- 10)
25   Casual Route
     (IV 10a, 7s) ★

traverse left to Table Ledge finishes (8) and exit to *Kiener's*, however, the route continues above. **P7:** Traverse right 15 feet, then climb a steep and exposed crack system to a sling belay below the right corner of a roof (11a, 100 feet). **P8:** Climb a right-facing dihedral to the top of the wall (9, 130 feet). Pro: SR plus an extra #2.5 through #4 Friend. FA: Layton Kor and Charlie Roskoz (V 5.8 A4), 1962. FFA: Dihedral on first pitch, Roger Briggs, 1976; of *A4 Traverse* on fifth pitch, Charlie Fowler and Dan Stone, 1978; of *Briggs-Candelaria* version, Roger Briggs and Rob Candelaria, 1976.

20a A4 Traverse (11b s)   From the fourth belay, climb a shallow, right-leaning, left-facing corner, then make a desperate traverse right with marginal pro to another shallow corner. Follow this up and right to a vertical crack that leads to a ledge in the Grand Traverse Dihedral. Belay here or climb to the Yellow Wall Bivouac Ledge (180 feet).

21   Black Dagger (V- 11a) ★   This unique route takes *D7* or *Yellow Wall* to Crossover Ledge, then continues straight up into the long, tapered chimney for which the route is named. Pro: SR plus many pieces from a half-inch to one-inch. FA: Wayne Goss and Roger Dalke (V 5.7 A3), 1966. FFA: Duncan Ferguson, 1980.

22   Forrest Finish (V- 10)   This direct route, which parallels *Black Dagger* on the right, comprised the first solo ascent of The Diamond. It ascends the first four pitches of *Yellow Wall*, then follows an independent crack system straight to the top of the face. FA: Bill Forrest, solo (V 5.7 A3), 1970.

23   Bright Star (V 10a A3) ★   This route is dedicated to the memory of Lauren Husted. It ascends five original pitches above the left side of the Broadway Bivouac Cave, follows a pitch each of *Grand Traverse* and *Yellow Wall* (*Casual Route*), then continues straight up the head wall above Table Ledge for two more difficult and dramatic pitches. The first ascent took three days. FA: Ed Webster, solo, 1984. FFA of first four pitches: Charlie Fowler and Scott Cosgrove in 1987. Pro: KBs to 4 inches with many small Stoppers and two sets of Friends.

24   Grand Traverse (V 8 A4)   This classic aid route is rarely climbed but for its central pitches which are overlapped by *Casual Route*. The name is derived from a 90-foot A4 traverse along Table Ledge. Begin just right of the Broadway Bivouac Cave. Pro: SR to a #4 Friend plus aid gear from RURPs and KBs. FA: Bob Boucher and Pat Ament, 1964. The two long pitches above Table Ledge may have been climbed free at 11b each.

24a Free Start (11b) ★   FFA: Bernard and Robert Gillett, 1992.

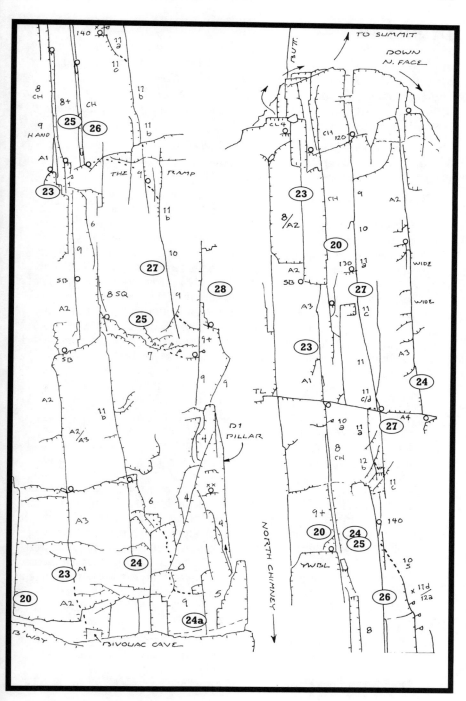

D1 PILLAR

The following five routes begin from a 180-foot, cone-shaped pillar just left of the North Chimney. Though there are at least three ways to climb the pillar, the usual method begins about 20 feet left of the North Chimney: Climb up and right along a left-facing corner, then go up and left to a belay ledge with a fixed anchor (5, 140 feet). There is another good ledge about 15 feet higher. A short easy pitch leads to the top.

The Ramp: About 200 feet above the top of the D1 Pillar, the wall curves back to form a large sloping ledge called The Ramp, which is intersected by Casual Route, Diamond Lil, Eroica, D1 and Jack of Diamonds.

25 **Casual Route (IV 10a, 7s) ★**   This climb was known as the *Integral Route* until it was free-soloed by Charlie Fowler about 1984. When asked what it was like to solo The Diamond, Charlie said, "Casual." *Casual Route* is the easiest line on The Diamond. It is always interesting and sustained in difficulty but at an easier level than the other free climbs. The route follows the right margin of the Yellow Wall area with the last pitch up to Table Ledge the crux. Note: There are several options for the arrangement of belays other than that shown in the topo. Begin at the D1 Pillar about 150 feet right of the Bivouac Cave and about 20 feet left of the North Chimney. **P1:** Climb a short left-facing corner, then work up and left to ledge with a fixed anchor (5, 140 feet). **P2:** Work up and left to the bottom of the D1 crack, then climb the crack for about 40 feet to a belay stance (9, 100 feet). **P3:** Traverse straight left, then angle up and left along flakes and small ledges to a stance at the bottom of a squeeze chimney (7, 100 feet). There are several fixed pins along this traverse. Do not start the traverse from the top of the D1 pillar, it is 10c with poor pro. **P4:** Climb the squeeze chimney, then continue up and slightly left to a belay in a big right-facing dihedral at the left end of The Ramp (8, 160 feet). **P5:** Climb the dihedral to a large grassy ledge (8+, 155 feet) or belay at a stance halfway up the corner. **P6:** A short (or long) pitch leads to the Yellow Wall Bivouac Ledge (6, 50 feet). **P7:** From the right side of the ledge, climb an inset (9+) followed by a narrow chimney (8), then pass a bulge with a fixed pin (crux) and belay at Table Ledge (10a, 130 feet). **P8:** Traverse left past fixed pins, then down a bit to Almost Table Ledge. Climb up and right past fixed pins to Table Ledge and traverse left to a left-facing dihedral with a fixed anchor and belay (8, 140 feet). Exit left and finish with *Kiener's*, or do the *Diamond Rappel Route* from Almost Table Ledge. FA: Duncan Ferguson and Chris Reveley, 1978.

26 **Diamond Lil (V 9 A3)**   The entire route except for the long chimney and dihedral above the left side of The Ramp has been climbed free as *Eroica*. FA: Michael Covington, Doug Scott and Dennis Henneck, 1976.

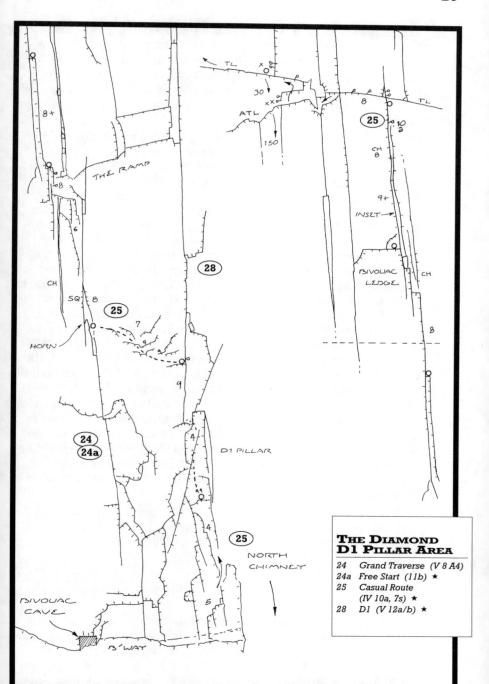

THE DIAMOND
D1 PILLAR AREA

24   Grand Traverse (V 8 A4)
24a Free Start (11b) ★
25   Casual Route
     (IV 10a, 7s) ★
28   D1 (V 12a/b) ★

27 Eroica (V+ 12b, *10s*) ★   Eroica is the name given to Beethoven's Third Symphony, though the route is named in memory of the late Eric Goukas. It is one of the best routes on The Diamond, generally safe but very challenging. It free climbs all of *Diamond Lil* but the long chimney and dihedral above the left side of The Ramp. Pro: SR with double RPs, Stoppers and TCUs. FA: Roger Briggs and Eric Doub, 1987.

28 D1 (V 12a/b) ★   Also known as the *Ace of Diamonds*, *D1* was the first route on The Diamond. It was one of the more difficult aid routes and is no piece of cake as a free climb. From the D1 Pillar, it follows a continuous crack system straight up the middle of the wall to the top. The crux and cleanest pitch is a shallow left-facing corner above Table Ledge. **P1:** Climb to the fixed belay on the D1 Pillar (5, 140 feet). **P2:** Continue to the top of the pillar, then follow a right-facing dihedral up and right and back left to a ledge (9, 150). The ledge also may be reached via the fingercrack on the second pitch of the *Casual Route* (9+). **P3:** Climb a right-facing dihedral and turn the roof at its top, then follow a crack to the top of The Ramp (10d, 150 feet). It is advantageous to belay on the next ledge above. This can be done with an additional short pitch (10a, 30 feet) or in one long lead with a 60-meter rope. **P4:** From the ledge above The Ramp, climb straight up the crack to a ledge on the right with two bolts (11a, 150 feet). **P5:** Continue up the crack system to an alcove at Table Ledge (10d, 100 feet). **P6a:** Step left and climb a difficult crack to a left-facing dihedral that is followed to a pedestal with a two-pin anchor (12a/b, 120 feet). **P6b:** Climb the wet and nasty chimney straight up from the alcove to the same stance (11, wet, 120 feet). **P7:** Climb the upper chimney to the top of the wall (9, wet or icy, 140 feet). Pro: SR plus extra pieces up to 3.5 inches. FA: Dave Rearick and Bob Kamps (V 5.7 A4), 1960. FFA: John Bachar and Billy Westbay, 1976 (via the wet chimney above Table Ledge). FFA of dihedral above Table Ledge: Roger Briggs and Jeff Achey, 1980.

29 Jack of Diamonds (V 9 A4)   This early aid line is rarely climbed and has not received a complete free ascent. The route runs parallel to *D1* about 50 to the right. It is very steep with a somewhat rotten midsection. The big right-facing dihedral below Table Ledge may have been climbed free at 10c. Begin at the top of the North Chimney in the corner that forms the right margin of the D1 Pillar. FA: Layton Kor and Royal Robbins, 1963.

30 Enos Mills Wall (V 7 A4 or 11c/d, unfinished)   The first ascent of this route was also the first winter ascent of The Diamond (climbed in early March). Now a classic aid route, it has repelled all free climbing attempts, however, the pitches up to the sling belay 30 feet below Table Ledge have been climbed free. The line follows a series

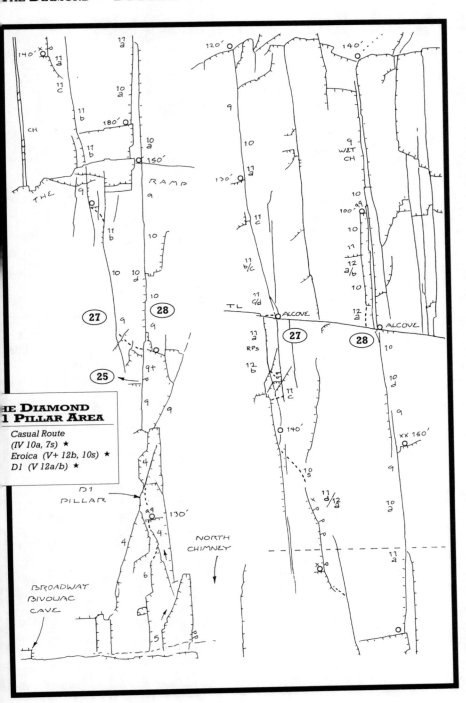

**THE DIAMOND
D1 PILLAR AREA**

*Casual Route
(IV 10a, 7s)* ★
Eroica (V+ 12b, 10s) ★
D1 (V 12a/b) ★

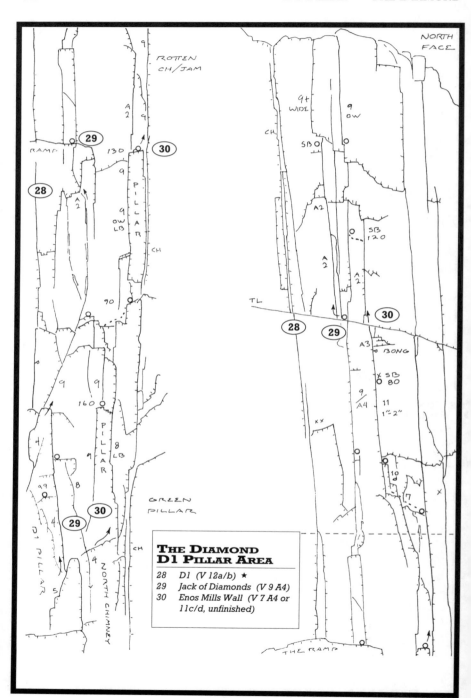

THE DIAMOND
D1 PILLAR AREA

28 D1 (V 12a/b) ★
29 Jack of Diamonds (V 9 A4)
30 Enos Mills Wall (V 7 A4 or
    11c/d, unfinished)

of steep dihedrals about 75 feet right of *D1*. Pro: Rack up to four inches. FA: Layton Kor and Wayne Goss, 1967. FFA through fifth pitch: Jeff Achey and Leonard Coyne, 1980.

30a Variation   Begin from the right side of the North Chimney at Broadway. Climb (mixed free and aid) up the left side of The Green Pillar for 180 feet. Where a chimney/ramp system veers off to the right, move left and climb to the top of a thin expanding flake. Mixed free and aid climbing leads to the bottom of the long flat pillar mentioned above. Climb a right-facing dihedral and chimney along the right side of the pillar (mostly free) and belay on top. Aid up a vertical wall for 80 feet, then pendulum left to a good crack that is climbed to a ledge on the regular route.

THE GREEN PILLAR

This 300-foot-high buttress sits across the North Chimney from the D1 Pillar and is the left and larger of three such features on the north side of the wall. The following four aid climbs begin from this pillar.

31 **La Dolce Vita (VI 8 A4)**   This is the Diamond section of an aid route that begins from Mills Glacier. It ascends the buttress just left of the North Chimney to reach Broadway, then continues up The Diamond directly above The Green Pillar. The lower section is described under the Lower East Face. Begin in a chimney along the left side of The Green Pillar. Pro: SR up to four inches plus Hooks, RURPs, KBs and many small angles. FA: Charlie Fowler and Renato Casaratto, 1984.

32 **Queen of Spades (V 8 A4)**   This is one of several aid lines on the right side of The Diamond that has received little attention from free climbers. Pro: Rack up to five inches; mostly nuts with a few pitons. Begin at the bottom of a chimney that splits the lower part of The Green Pillar. FA: Mark Hesse and Doug Snively, 1974.

33 **Gear and Clothing (V 9 A4)**   This route gains the top of The Green Pillar, then goes straight up the wall just right of *La Dolce Vita*. Begin toward the right side of The Green Pillar. Pro: 5 KBs, 10 LAs, angles up to 1.25 inches, 15 wired Stoppers, 3 sets of Friends, a six-inch piece, 50 carabiners and 40 hero loops. FA: Kyle Copeland and Marc Hirt, 1985.

34 **Dunn-Westbay (V 8 A3)**   This route ascends the gigantic right-facing dihedral along the right side of The Green Pillar, then continues straight up the wall. Begin on the right side of The Green Pillar. Pro: SR to three inches plus KBs, hooks and quarter-inch bolt hangers. FA: Jimmy Dunn and Billy Westbay, 1972.

34a Tail of the Tiger (A3)   From the top of The Green Pillar, start the fourth pitch of the *Dunn-Westbay*, then aid up and right along a crack and curvilinear roof to *King of Swords*. FA: Kris Walker and Walt Walker, 1973.

35 King of Swords (V 12a, 11a s) ★   Except for the first two pitches which are original, this is the free version of the aid climb *Its Welx*. It is one of the finest routes on The Diamond. Be prepared for continuously difficult climbing, phenomenal exposure and a bit of poor rock. Begin at the right side of The Green Pillar, beneath the first major crack system right of the *Dunn-Westbay* dihedral. **P1:** Climb 90 feet up to a vertical right-facing dihedral and follow it to a stance (10a, 120 feet). **P2:** Follow the corner for another 60 feet, then work up and right for 50 feet to a pedestal above a right-facing dihedral (10d, 150 feet). **P3:** This pitch navigates a rotten recess called the Torture Chamber and is the most intimidating of the climb. Step right into the main crack (*Its Welx*) and climb to where it goes offwidth. Move left (11d) and climb a crack for 25 feet (11a s), then work back into the main crack and climb to a tiny stance (11d, 100 feet). **P4:** Climb straight up a fist crack past a roof to a stance (11, 150 feet). **P5:** Work straight up until it is possible to move left on flakes and gain a clean fingercrack that forms the left side of a long pillar. Climb the crack and belay atop the pillar (11c/d, 100 feet). **P6:** Climb a handcrack to Table Ledge and continue for about 40 feet, then traverse left and belay (11d, 140 feet). **P7:** Climb a steep crack with a difficult slot, then shoot straight for the top of the wall passing some small roofs along the way (11, 140 feet). Pro: Double SR with three #1 to #2.5 Friends. FA of first two pitches and FFA of pitches three through seven: Roger Briggs and Dan Stone, 1985.

35a Gilbert Variation (11d) ★   From **P4:** Step right into the main crack but continue up the gaping offwidth section (11a s). **P5:** Climb the super-clean dihedral along the right side of the pillar until it is possible to move left and continue to the top of the pillar (11d, 100 feet). FA: Mike Gilbert.

36 Smash the State (V 8 A5)   It takes your money without your consent, spends it on things you don't want, then tells you what you can and cannot do. Now why would anyone want to Smash the State? Though I have a rough topo of this route apparently drawn by Jim Beyer, it is difficult tell exactly where it goes. It begins in the recess between The Green Pillar and Black Flake Pillar, then wanders back and forth between *King of Swords* and *The Joker*. It appears to take the left-hand version on the fifth pitch of *King of Swords* and then continues with that route to the top of the wall. FA: Jim Beyer, solo, 1989.

**THE DIAMOND
GREEN PILLAR
AREA**

30	*Enos Mills Wall (V 7 A4 or 11c/d, unfinished)*
31	*La Dolce Vita (VI 8 A4)*
32	*Queen of Spades (V 8 A4)*
33	*Gear and Clothing (V 9 A4)*
34	*Dunn-Westbay (V 8 A3)*
34a	*Tail of the Tiger (A3)*
35	*King of Swords (V 12a, 11a s) ★*

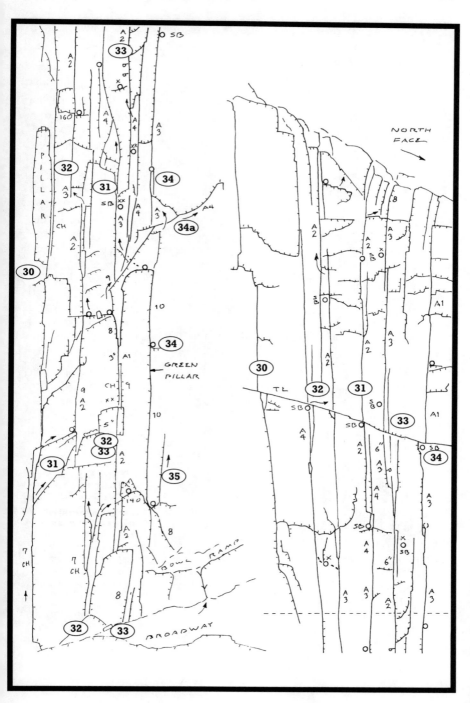

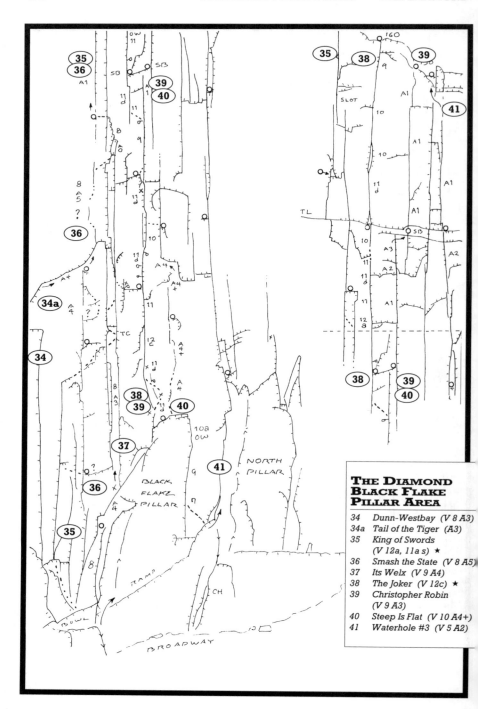

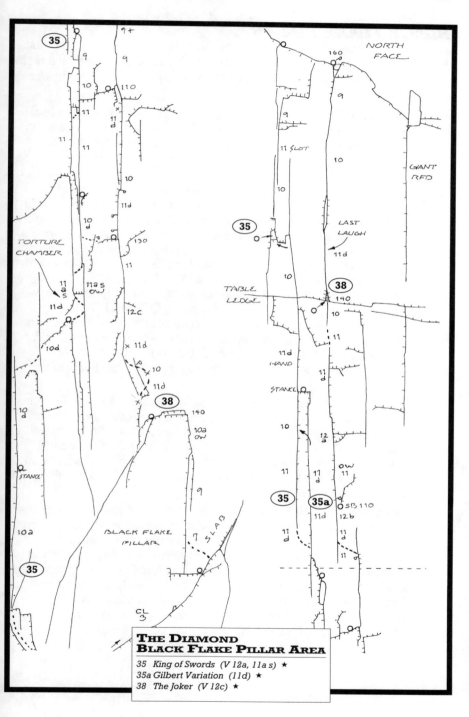

**THE DIAMOND
BLACK FLAKE PILLAR AREA**

35   *King of Swords (V 12a, 11a s)* ★
35a *Gilbert Variation (11d)* ★
38   *The Joker (V 12c)* ★

BLACK FLAKE PILLAR

This small buttress sits across a gap to the north from The Green Pillar and has a flat and narrow black face. It is 150 feet high and is accessed by a ramp that angles up and right along its base. The following four routes begin from this feature.

37 **Its Welx (V 9 A4)**   This very difficult aid route begins in the recess between The Green Pillar and the Black Flake Pillar. Except for the first two pitches, the route has been climbed free under the name *King of Swords* (above). FA: Dan McClure and Mark Hesse, 1973.

38 **The Joker (V 12c)** ★   This route free climbs the first three-and-a-half pitches of *Christopher Robin*, then switches to a previously unclimbed crack on the left and continues straight to the top of wall. It is, at time of writing, the hardest free climb on The Diamond. Begin at the alcove below *King of Swords* and scramble up and right along a ramp to the bottom of a big right-facing dihedral that forms the right side of the Black Flake Pillar. Pro: Medium RPs to large Stoppers, two sets #0.5 to #3 Friends, plus a #3.5 and #4 Friend. Pitches 2 and 3 have many fixed nuts and require only a #0.5 to #3 Friend with two #2 Friends on the second pitch, plus many QDs. FA/FFA: Roger Briggs and Steve Levin (with the addition of several bolts, fixed pins and nuts) took several falls on three pitches and used two points of aid passing The Last Laugh above Table Ledge, 1993. The first complete free ascent was made by Roger Briggs and Pat Adams, 1994.

39 **Christopher Robin (V 9 A3)**   This spectacular aid route ascends the overhanging wall about 30 feet right of *King of Swords*. It was assumed that *The Joker* free climbed the entire line of *Christopher Robin*, but after reviewing the routes with Kris Walker, it became apparent that they diverge halfway up the fourth pitch. Begin as for *The Joker*. Pro: Rack up to a #4 Friend with an assortment of thin pitons. FA: Kris Walker, solo, 1972.

40 **Steep Is Flat (V 10 A4+)**   This route climbs the steep wall between *Christopher Robin* and *Waterhole #3* to arrive at the bivouac ledge for *Christopher Robin*. The upper part of the route appears to be largely the same as *Christopher Robin* except that Beyer switched to a crack on the right about 30 feet from the top. The line of the route shown in the topo is based on Beyer's sketch and is approximate. Pro: SR to four inches plus 20 copperheads, 10 KBs, 6 LAs, two angles each up to 0.75 inch, 7 beaks and a double set of hooks. FA: Jim Beyer and Pat McInerney, 1990.

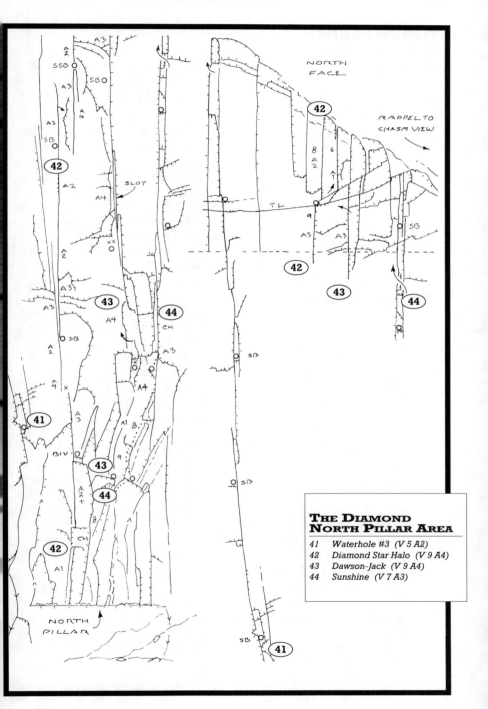

THE DIAMOND NORTH PILLAR AREA

41	Waterhole #3 *(V 5 A2)*
42	Diamond Star Halo *(V 9 A4)*
43	Dawson-Jack *(V 9 A4)*
44	Sunshine *(V 7 A3)*

NORTH PILLAR

This is the farthest right of three buttresses to the right of the North Chimney. It is shaped somewhat like an owl and is higher than the Black Flake Pillar. About 200 feet above the North Pillar, two curvilinear streaks of dark rock known as The Horsetails sweep up to the right and aid in locating features on the following routes.

41 Waterhole #3 (V 5 A2)   This aid route ascends the left side of the North Pillar, then sweeps up and left in a continuous crack system that leads to an enormous roof at the top of the wall. It was the first route on the right side of The Diamond and the first solo ascent of a completely new route. Bill Forrest made the first solo ascent of The Diamond in 1970, but the first two-thirds of his route followed *Yellow Wall*. Scramble up a ramp to gain the recess between the Black Flake Pillar and the North Pillar. The route described utilizes the fewest possible belays; the first ascent took three days and required ten pitches due to an inadequate rack. Pro: SR plus an assortment of pitons (mostly thin). FA: Kris Walker, solo, 1971.

42 Diamond Star Halo (V 9 A4)   This spectacular aid route ascends the North Pillar, then goes straight up the overhanging wall through the right side of The Horsetails. The wall leans out so far that water dripping from the top falls 15 feet free of the lower face. When the cracks fizzle out, a double pendulum affords access to a left-facing dihedral system that leads to the top of the wall. Scramble onto a ledge at the bottom of the North Pillar and set the first belay at a left-facing dihedral. Pro: 12 KBs, 12 LAs, five each angles up to one inch, 4 each 1.25- and 1.5-inch angles, two 2-inch angles, two 3-inch angles, assorted hooks, 15 bashies, a few RURPs, many wired nuts, several Tri-cams up to #7 and three complete sets of Friends. FA: Charlie Fowler, Kyle Copeland and Joe Burke, 1986.

43 Dawson-Jack (V 9 A4)   This very difficult route ascends the long, left-facing dihedral at the far right side of The Diamond. Begin up on a ledge at the right side of the North Pillar and beneath a right-leaning chimney about 30 feet right of Diamond Star Halo. Pro: SR to three inches plus RURPs, hooks and many pitons. FA: Lou Dawson and R. Jack, 1975.

44 Sunshine (V 7 A3)   Fifty feet right of the long left-facing dihedral of *Dawson-Jack*, a long right-facing dihedral leads to a gigantic roof. Sunshine follows the latter dihedral and climbs out the left side of the roof. Begin toward the right side of the long grassy ledge that runs beneath the North Pillar, a short way right of the wet chimney of the preceding route. Pro: Augmented SR plus hooks and pins from KBs to four inches. FA: Jim Beyer, solo, 1973.

UPPER CHASM VIEW WALL

The following routes begin from the north end of Broadway and ascend the banded wall just right of The Diamond.

45 V-Notch Exit (II 7) ★   This is the easiest way to reach Chasm View from Broadway. Traverse north along Broadway and identify a distinct V-notch on the skyline about 200 feet right of *Chasm View*. Continue past the *Chasm View* rappels and scramble up ramps and ledges until directly beneath the notch. Climb a steep chimney and crack system that lead to the notch in a single pitch, then walk through to the talus slope on the north side. FA: Roger Briggs.

46 Chasm Cut-Off (II 7)   This ancient route follows a ledge system along the lowest band of schist that runs across the top of Chasm View Wall and provides an escape from Broadway. From the north end of Broadway, follow a narrowing, grassy ledge system that traverses out over Chasm View Wall. Pass a small corner and an undercut area. Eventually the ledge fades and one is confronted with a small overhang; climb this directly by pulling on a fixed pin. Traverse right a ways, climb a flake and step around onto the ridge crest. FA: Bill Eubank, Tom Hornbein and Brad Van Diver, 1950.

*Derek Hersey on Yellow Wall,
free solo. Photo: Steve Bartlett.*

INDEX

Bolded numbers refer to topos or photos of the feature or route.